GO
Green

Wonderful
Water

Helen Lanz

SEA-TO-SEA
Mankato Collingwood London

This edition first published in 2012 by

Sea-to-Sea Publications
Distributed by Black Rabbit Books
P.O. Box 3263, Mankato, Minnesota 56002

Printed in China

9 8 7 6 5 4 3 2

Published by arrangement with the Watts
Publishing Group Ltd, London.

Library of Congress Cataloging-in-Publication Data

Lanz, Helen.
 Wonderful water / by Helen Lanz.
   p. cm. -- (Go green)
 Includes index.
 ISBN 978-1-59771-306-1 (library binding)
 1. Water conservation--Juvenile literature. 2. Water use--
Juvenile literature. 3. Water supply--Juvenile literature. I. Title.
 TD495.L36 2012
 333.91'16--dc22
                                        2011004380

Series Editor: Julia Bird
Design: D.R. ink
Art director: Jonathan Hair
Artworks: Mike Phillips

Picture credits: G M B Akash/Panos: 15b; Georgios
Alexandris/istockphoto: 17; Mikhail Bistrov/istockphoto: 27;
Cristiano Burmester/Alamy: 13b; Caro/Alamy: 11; Anthony
Cooper/Ecoscene: 22; T Costin/ istockphoto: 21t;Claudia
Dewald/istockphoto: 6b; Chad Ehlers/Alamy: 13t; EPA: 19t;The
Garden PL/Alamy: 23b; Bill Grove/istockphoto: 25b;Chris
Hepburn/istockphoto: 18l; Hippo The Water Saver ®: 21b;Ian
Hubball/istockphoto: front cover b; Image Source Pink/Alamy: 6t;
Bonnie Jacobs/istockphoto: 23t; Selina Joiner/istockphoto:
20;Thammarat Kaosombat/istockphoto: 10; Ethan
Myerson/istockphoto: 18r;Picture Partners/Alamy: 26t;
Giacomo Pirozzi/Panos: front cover t;Ragnarock/Shutterstock: 9t;
Recycle Now Partners: 26b; Ravi Tahilramani/istockphoto:15t;
Bridgit Taylor/DV/Getty Images: 16t; D Timiraos/istockphoto: 12;
Tishi/Shutterstock: 9b; Ken Welsh/Alamy: 25t; Peng
Wu/istockphoto: 24; Tania Zbrodko/Shutterstock: 16b;
Andrejs Zemdeya/istockphoto: 7.

To my mom because you're the stars in the sky and so on.

February 2011
RD/6000006415/001

"*During 25 years of writing about the environment for the Guardian, I quickly realized that education was the first step to protecting the planet on which we all depend for survival. While the warning signs are everywhere that the Earth is heating up and the climate changing, many of us have been too preoccupied with living our lives to notice what is going on in our wider environment. It seems to me that it is children who need to know what is happening—they are often more observant of what is going on around them. We need to help them to grow up respecting and preserving the natural world on which their future depends. By teaching them about the importance of water, energy, and other key areas of life, we can be sure they will soon be influencing their parents' lifestyles, too. This is a series of books every child should read.*"

Paul Brown
Former environment correspondent for the UK's *Guardian* newspaper, environmental author, and fellow of Wolfson College, Cambridge, UK.

Contents

Words in **bold** can be found in the glossary on page 28.

Water for Life

What have you done today? Have you had a soft drink, or brushed your teeth? Maybe you've been for a bike ride? Many of the things you've done today will have used water in some way, from turning the faucet on to get a drink, to making the bike you're riding.

Drinking plenty of water helps to keep us healthy and alert. You should drink more water when you've been exercising.

Drink to Survive

The most important use of water is for drinking. We cannot survive without drinking water. Children should drink between six and eight glasses of water every day. This helps your body to work properly, keeps you healthy, and helps you to concentrate. Plants and animals rely on fresh water for life, too.

Did you know?

Elephants can smell water from a distance of around 3 miles (5 km) away.

 Just like people and animals, all plants need water to survive.

An Important Ingredient

We don't just need water to drink, cook, or wash in, we need it to make nearly everything we use, too. Water is needed to grow the foods we eat and to grow natural **materials**, such as cotton, used to make many of our clothes. It is also used in many of the processes to make things from beverage cans to the bricks we use to build our homes.

IT'S ALL ABOUT WATER

- **At birth, water makes up approximately 80 percent of a baby's body weight.**
- **Our brain is 75 percent water.**
- **80 percent of the contents of a pineapple and 95 percent of the contents of a tomato are water.**

95%

What Goes Around

Did you know there is the same amount of water in the world today as when the Earth was formed over 4.5 billion years ago? The water on our planet is always on the move in what is known as the **water cycle**.

The Water Cycle

2. These drops of water form clouds.

3. The water droplets in the clouds collect together and get bigger and heavier then fall as rain, sleet, or snow.

1. Water in rivers, lakes, and seas is heated by the Sun and turns into **water vapor**, or drops of water in the air.

4. The rain falls to the ground and runs back into rivers, lakes, and seas, and the cycle begins all over again.

Did you know?

We drink the same water now as the dinosaurs did more than 200 million years ago. That means that you have shared a drink with the dinosaurs!

Cheers!

A Watery World

Seventy percent of the Earth's surface is covered in water. But 97 percent of this is in the seas and oceans, so it is too salty for us to drink.

This picture of the Earth from space shows the blue seas and oceans.

GO GREEN!

Distribution of the world's water:

97% seawater

2% **ice caps** and **glaciers**

1% freshwater

Water is used for growing food all around the world.

Freshwater

Freshwater makes up just one percent of the Earth's water. People depend on it for drinking, washing in, for **industry** or the processes used to make things, **agriculture**, and many other uses.

Where Water Goes

Although our water goes around in a loop, there are many more demands made on it today than in the past. We are using up our freshwater supplies more quickly than the water cycle can refill them.

What water is used for:

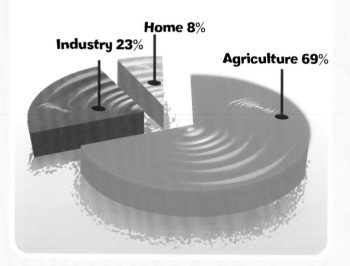

Industry 23%
Home 8%
Agriculture 69%

Food and Water

Growing food uses by far the largest amount of our freshwater. The world's **population** has exploded in the last 100 years, growing from 1.2 billion people in 1900 to more than six billion by 2000. That's a lot of mouths to feed!

Rice is usually grown in paddy fields. Rice needs a lot of water to make it grow, so the fields are often flooded by farmers.

Did you know?

Growing 2 pounds (1 kg) of rice uses up about 378 gallons (1,432 l) of water—the same as 18 full bathtubs!

- Despite the fact that Australia's rainfall is the lowest of all the continents in the world (except Antarctica), Australians use more water per person than anywhere else in the world.

- Producing the food eaten by the average American each year takes the same amount of water as filling almost three Olympic-sized swimming pools with water per person!

Fashion and Industry

The world's growing population uses more and more things, from clothes and toys to homes and transportation. Industry uses up the next largest amount of water after agriculture. It takes 2,000 gallons (8,000 l) of water (enough to fill 100 bathtubs) to make just one pair of leather shoes, for example.

Water in the Home

At home we use water for drinking, washing, cooking, and so on. In **developed countries** (the U.S., Australia, and the UK, for example), our water is cleaned before and after we use it. This is expensive and uses a lot of **energy**.

 Water is used in almost all industries, including the metalworking industry, where it is used for cooling.

Water Footprint

Have you ever thought about your **water footprint**? No—not the footprint you leave on the bath mat—the amount of water you use!

Direct and Indirect

Here's how a water footprint works. We use water in two ways: direct, or actual use, such as when we turn on the faucet or flush the toilet, and indirect use. This is the hidden amount of water that we don't use ourselves, but has been used to make or grow what we use or eat.

Down the Drain

On average, every person in the developed world uses about 40 gallons (150 l) of direct water a day to eat, drink, and wash in (that's nearly two full bathtubs); but nearly 30 times as much again in indirect water. That's the same as flushing the toilet more than 774 times in one day!

Imagine filling your bathtub more than 50 times in one day. That's about the same amount as your water footprint.

Someone Else's Water

Our water footprint may not only be large, it may also cover a huge distance. Often things we eat, drink, or use in this country have been made a long way away, using up water that may be in short supply in someone else's country.

 These people in Zimbabwe, in Africa, are tending to rows of crops. The crops will be sold all over the world.

CASE STUDY # MAKING A BEVERAGE CAN

 Sugarcane is used to make sugar. Growing and processing it uses up lots of water.

A beverage can may contain only 12 fluid ounces (0.35 l) of water, but it uses about 53 gallons (200 l) to grow the sugar that's in the drink and another 80 gallons (305 l) to make the can. The beverage is the direct amount, the water used to grow the sugar and make the can is the indirect amount.

A Changing Climate

How we choose to live affects our **environment**. If we use a lot of water at home, travel a lot in cars or planes, or buy lots of new things, it doesn't just cost us money, it costs the environment, too.

The Cost of Living

We rely on burning the **fossil fuels**—coal, oil, and gas—to produce energy in order to make things, grow things, keep our homes light and warm, or cook our food. The world's growing population is using more and more energy and this is having an impact on the world's climate.

2. The Earth has a layer of protective gases around it called the atmosphere. It allows the Sun's rays in, but also keeps in some of the Sun's heat. As more fuel is used, more greenhouse gases are added to the atmosphere. They are good at trapping heat, so more heat is kept in, warming the Earth up.

3. Rising temperatures have started to change the weather patterns around the world. This is called **climate change**.

1. Coal, oil, and gas develop underground over millions of years. When they are burned, they create energy. Burning these fuels gives off a gas called carbon dioxide, which is a **greenhouse gas**.

Warming Up

The Earth's climate varies naturally, but people have made it change more quickly by burning more and more fossil fuels. We can already see the effects of climate change—some areas have hardly any rain, while others have too much. It is predicted that as more greenhouse gases go into the air, the Earth's climate will warm up further, and some countries will become even drier. If this happens, our water will become even more precious.

As our climate changes, where it was once possible to grow food or live safely is changing, too, due to **drought** (above) and **floods** (right).

Did you know?

Four out of every ten people in the world are not able to get to clean water easily.

In the Kitchen

The good news is that it is easy to save water every day. And what's even better is that if we all do it, we can make even bigger savings.

Chill!

Did you know that every time you run the faucet waiting for the water to run cold to get a cold drink, you waste more than 2 gallons (9 l) of water a minute? That is nearly a whole bucket of water down the drain. Instead of doing that, just fill up a jug with water and put it in the refrigerator.

It takes a lot of water and energy to make a can.

Water kept in the refrigerator is cold and refreshing.

A Healthy Choice

Next time you are thirsty, instead of reaching for a canned or bottled beverage, just drink a glass of water. Not only is this much more healthy than drinking a canned beverage, it is much better for the environment, too, because you're not using a can or bottle. Remember, it takes water to make these as well as fill them.

FAUCET FACTS

- On average, a family in the United States will turn the faucet on between 70–100 times a day.

- In the UK in the 1830s, each person used about 5 gallons (18 l) of water a day; by 1930, this had risen to 33 gallons (126 l). Today, it is about 40 gallons (150 l) a day.

Two for the Price of One!

If you are boiling vegetables, try to just cover them with water. Any more is a waste!

Who does the cooking in your house? Remind them to use only the amount of water needed when it comes to cooking vegetables or boiling the tea kettle. This not only saves on water, but also on the energy needed to make the water boil.

Lighten the Load

There is more good news! We can save water at home when we do the dishes and the laundry, too.

Doing the Dishes

Many homes now have a dishwasher. So which is best—washing by hand or using a dishwasher? A dishwasher uses about 4 gallons (15 l) of water compared to a sink, which holds about 2 gallons (8 l). But if you wash dishes by hand a few times during the day, you can end up using more water than is used in the dishwasher.

 Research has shown that washing the dishes by hand doesn't always save water.

As long as you scrape, but don't rinse, the plates first, and wait until the dishwasher is full before turning it on, studies have shown that using the right dishwasher saves both water and energy.

SAVING ENERGY

If you need a new appliance, such as a dishwasher or washing machine, talk to your mom or dad about choosing one that is energy efficient. Look at the labels, such as the Energy Star or the Energy Saving Recommended labels. These show which appliances use less water and energy, and so will be better for the environment.

Clean Clothes

Each time you turn on the washing machine, it uses about 25 gallons (95 l) of water (that's about 380 glasses!) so only put your clothes in to be washed when they need it. And as with the dishwasher, turn the washing machine on only when it is full.

Did you know?

Using an energy-efficient washing machine can save more water in one year than one person drinks in their whole lifetime!

I'm just going to wear my clothes one more time.

I don't think they need to be *that* dirty!

Bathroom Basics

There are lots of things you can do to save water in the bathroom—and still get clean!

Turn It Off

Do you leave the faucet running when you brush your teeth? That sends 2 gallons (9 l) of water down the drain every minute. If you brush your teeth for three minutes (the way you should), that's 7 gallons (27 l) of water wasted each time you brush your teeth. Save that over a week, and you'll have enough water to splash around in an inflatable pool.

Turn the faucet off every time you brush your teeth. It will save enough water to splash in the pool on a sunny day!

HOW MUCH?

 Taking a bath uses around 21 gallons (80 l) of water.

Taking a shower uses 1.5 gallons (5 l) of water per minute. A power shower can use up to 3 gallons (10 l) of water a minute.

 Flushing the toilet uses up to 2.5 gallons (9 l) of water—more than half a bucketful.

Don't Soak!

Running a bath can use much more water than taking a shower, unless you have a power shower. If you have a five-minute shower instead of a bath, you can save about 14.5 gallons (55 l) of water. That's enough to make about 220 cups of coffee!

 Only some showers save water. A power shower can use up to three times more water than having a bath.

CASE STUDY # FEELING FLUSH

Did you know that we probably flush away as much water in a day as we drink in a whole month? Old-fashioned single-flush toilets use up to about 2.3 gallons (9 l) of water a flush; modern dual-flush toilets use up to 1.5 gallons (6 l). If you have an old-fashioned toilet, see if you can install a water-saving device like a Water Hippo™. Or just fill up an empty drinks bottle with water and put that in your cistern.

The Water Hippo™ fits in the toilet cistern, taking up space so that less water is needed for each flush.

Saving Water Outside

A lot of water wasted in the home is actually wasted outside—in the yard or washing the car.

Storing Water

Have you got a **rain barrel** outside? This can collect up to 1,320 gallons (5,000 l) of rainwater a year—enough water to fill ten medium-sized inflatable pools. You can use this to water both indoor and outdoor plants when the weather is dry.

Remember to put a lid on your rain barrel. This keeps the water clean and stops leaves from falling into it.

Did you know?

A lawn sprinkler left to water the grass for an hour can use as much water as a family of four does in one entire day.

Hide the Hose

If you help to wash the car, be sure to do it with a plastic pail and sponge, rather than a hose. Hoses can use up to 265 gallons (1,000 l) of water an hour—that's enough to fill 12.5 bathtubs. You can save water by using water from your rain barrel instead of the faucet.

Thanks So Mulch!

Have you ever heard of mulch? It's a mixture of wet grass or bark and leaves. If you have a garden or vegetable patch, it can be put around your plants to keep the soil damp. It means you don't have to water your garden as often, and so is another good way to save water.

▲ Washing the car with a pail and sponge can save a lot of water.

▼ A layer of mulch helps to keep soil moist.

Down the Drain!

It is a good idea to look around your home for drips and leaks—repairing these can save a lot of water.

Remember to turn the faucet off completely when you have finished using it.

Drip, Drip, Drip

A dripping faucet can waste more than 24 gallons (90 l) of water a week—that's more than a bathtub full. If you find a faucet or pipe is leaking, tell your mom or dad so that they can fix it or call a plumber.

Every Bit Helps

Save used dishwater from the kitchen by pouring it into a watering can. Rather than pouring it down the sink, use it to water any house plants or flowers in the garden.

Did you know?
A dripping faucet can waste up to a bucketful of water a day.

Careful Cleaning

Be careful about what goes down the drain. Any fluids you wash away join the water system, so put down as few **chemicals** as possible. If you help with the grocery shopping, look for cleaning products that are eco-friendly—these are designed to be kinder to the environment.

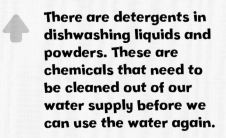

There are detergents in dishwashing liquids and powders. These are chemicals that need to be cleaned out of our water supply before we can use the water again.

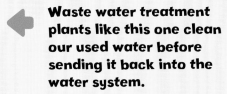

Waste water treatment plants like this one clean our used water before sending it back into the water system.

LEAKY FACTS

- If every household in the United States had a faucet that leaked one drop every second, it would add up to enough wasted water to fill 1,687 Olympic swimming pools a day!

- By repairing a faucet so it doesn't drip anymore, you could save up to 1,450 gallons (5,500 l) of water a year—that's nearly 69 full bathtubs.

Pass On a Glass!

Have you heard of the three Rs—reduce, reuse, recycle? That is just what we need to do with our water.

Step-by-Step

First, we need to reduce how much water we use to help save it in the first place. We can reuse it in our homes and yards to water plants instead of letting it run down the drain. When possible, we can buy things made from **recycled** materials, which often uses much less water than making something from scratch.

Use the dirty dishwater to water the plants in your backyard.

CASE STUDY

PAPER

It saves at least 8,000 gallons (30,000 l) of water (a milk tanker's worth) to make one ton of recycled paper, instead of making paper from new materials. It also saves enough energy to run a three-bedroom house for one year and reduces the amount of air pollution by 95 percent. That has got to be a win-win situation!

You can help recycle paper by making sure that there are no staples or plastics mixed in with the paper you are recycling.

Water is a precious resource that helps to make our Earth as beautiful as it is.

Small Changes, Big Difference

Make small changes to how you use water every day. Remember, even a small change, if we all make it, will make a big difference. We need to make good choices so we can preserve our water and ensure that your children can share a drink with a dinosaur, too!

Glossary

Agriculture Farming.

Chemicals Something that has been made through a chemical process. For example, detergents are chemicals that clean by removing dirt particles.

Climate change Long-term changes to the Earth's weather patterns.

Developed countries Countries that are wealthy and rely on money from industry; and where most people work in factories and businesses rather than agriculture.

Drought Where there is a shortage of rain over a long period of time.

Dual-flush A toilet that has two buttons so you can flush with a full cistern of water or part-cistern, to save water.

Energy This is the power needed to make or do something. Electricity is a form of energy.

Environment Surroundings.

Fossil fuels Fuels, such as coal, oil, or gas, that have developed under the ground from rotting animal and plant life over millions of years.

Glaciers A very slow-moving mass of ice that has formed over many years by layers of snow building up on top of each other and hardening.

Greenhouse gas Carbon dioxide and methane are greenhouse gases. They create an invisible layer around the Earth, trapping in the heat of the Sun's rays.

Ice caps A layer of ice and snow that covers a large area of land all year round.

Industry Factories and businesses that make things.

Materials What something is made from, such as cotton, wood, or metal.

Population The number of people living in a place.

Rain barrel A container to catch and store rainwater.

Recycle To process a product so that the materials that it is made from can be used again.

Water cycle The way our water supply moves throughout our environment.

Water footprint The amount of water a person, company, or country uses per day. It is made up of direct water use—the water we drink, cook with, or wash with—and indirect water use—the water that has been used to make the things we buy or use.

Water vapor Tiny water droplets in the air that form together to make clouds.

Useful Information

Throughout this book, "real-life measurements" are used for reference. These measurements are not exact, but give a sense of just how much an amount of water is, or what it looks like.

1 cup or glass full = 8 FLUID OUNCES (0.25 L)

1 bucketful = 4 GALLONS (14 L)

1 full bathtub = 21 GALLONS (80 L)

1 average inflatable pool = 130 GALLONS (495 L)

1 milk tanker = 7,925 GALLONS (30,000 L)

Olympic-size pool = 660,430 GALLONS (2,500,000 L)

Further Reading

Earth Watch: Water for All by Sally Morgan (Franklin Watts, 2005)

Green Team: Using Water by Sally Hewitt (Franklin Watts, 2008)

Exploring Earth's Resources by Sharon Katz Cooper (Heinemann, 2007)

Web Sites

http://kids.nationalgeographic.com/ kids/games/puzzlesquizzes/
Quiz yourself about water to see how much you know about it!

http://water.epa.gov/
Click on Education & Training and then Kids to discover fun games and activities that will teach you about water.

www.wateraid.org
A worldwide charity that aims to bring clean water to everyone.

Dates to Remember

World Water Day—March 22
Set up by the United Nations in 1993, it is a day to think about how we use water and our global water resources. Visit www.worldwaterday.org.

World Food Day—October 16
Set up by the Food and Agriculture Organization (FAO), part of the United Nations, in 1979 to draw attention to world food shortages. Visit www.fao.org.

Index